The Big Book of
PLANES

REVISED EDITION

Assistant editor Debangana Banerjee
Editor Ishani Nandi
Art editor Shipra Jain
Senior editors Marie Greenwood, Shatarupa Chaudhuri
Senior art editors Jim Green, Nishesh Batnagar
DTP designers Bimlesh Tiwary, Syed Md Farhan
Managing editors Laura Gilbert, Alka Thakur Hazarika
Managing art editors Diane Peyton Jones,
Romi Chakraborty
CTS manager Balwant Singh
Production manager Pankaj Sharma
Producer, pre-production Nadine King
Picture researcher Aditya Katyal
Publisher Sarah Larter
Jacket designers Kartik Gera, Dheeraj Arora
Additional text Reg Grant
Consultant Reg Grant

ORIGINAL EDITION

Written and edited by Lorrie Mack
Designers Cheryl Telfer, Helen Chapman
Publishing manager Sue Leonard
Managing art editor Clare Shedden
Jacket design Chris Drew
Picture researcher Sarah Stewart-Richardson
Production Shivani Pandey
DTP designer Almudena Díaz
DTP assistant Pilar Morales
Consultant Ben Morgan

First published in Great Britain in 2004
This edition first published in Great Britain in 2016
by Dorling Kindersley Limited
80 Strand, London, WC2R 0RL

Copyright © 2004, 2016
Dorling Kindersley Limited
A Penguin Random House Company

2 4 6 8 10 9 7 5 3 1
001–321334–May/2020

ISBN 978-0-2414-6181-5
Printed and bound in China

A WORLD OF IDEAS:
SEE ALL THERE IS TO KNOW
www.dk.com

Dorling Kindersley would like to thank: Kristin Snow at Air Tractor, Inc., Olney, Texas; Jack Brown's Seaplane Base, Florida; Dan Sweet at Columbia Helicopters, Portland, Oregon; Major Mike Chapa and John Haire at Edwards Air Force base, California; Fantasy of Flight, Florida; Chris Finnigan, BMAA, Oxfordshire; Ellen Bendell at Lockheed Martin, Palmdale, California; Beth Hagenauer at NASA Dryden Flight Research Center, Edwards, California; Nancy Machado and Duane Swing at Velocity Inc, Sebastian, Florida. The publisher would like to thank the following for their kind permission to reproduce their photographs. **Position key:** c=center; b=bottom; l=left; r=right; t=top. **3 Alamy Images:** Stocktrek Images, Inc. / Andrew Chittock (crb). **Corbis:** Transtock / Robert Kerian (cr). **4-5 Getty Images:** Science & Society Picture Library (c). **5 Alamy Images:** LOC Photo (bc); Paul Briden (crb). **Getty Images:** Science & Society Picture Library (tr). **6 Donald Browning:** (tl). **8 NASA:** (tl). **10 NASA:** (cla). **10-11 Deutsche Lufthansa AG.** **11 Getty Images:** AFP / Mark RALSTON (tl); Bloomberg / Chris Ratcliffe (cr). **12 123RF.com:** Thomas Dutour (clb). **Alamy Images:** AV8 Collection 2 (tl). **12-13 Dreamstime.com:** Ermess (b). **13 Dreamstime.com:** Micka (tc). **14 Air Tractor inc:** (clb). **16-17 Velocity Inc:** (All images on the spread). **18 E.J. Koningsveld:** (b). **Plane Picture Company:** John M. Dibbs (t). **18-19 E.J. Koningsveld:** (b). **19 The Flight Collection:** Quadrant Picture Library / Chris Bennett (br). **Plane Picture Company:** John M. Dibbs (c). **20 NASA:** Jim Ross (tl). **21 NASA:** Tony Landis (cr). **22-23 Dorling Kindersley:** RAF Battle of Britain Memorial Flight (c). **iStockphoto.com:** Andy_Oxley (b). **22 Dreamstime.com:** VanderWolf Images (tl). **23 iStockphoto.com:** Andy_Oxley (tr). **24 P&M Aviation:** (tl). **26 Alamy Images:** TRISTAR PHOTOS (cl). **26-27 Alamy Images:** i car (b); Chris Laurens (c). **27 Alamy Images:** Peter Titmuss (tc). **28-29 Alamy Images:** MERVYN REES (b). **28 NASA:** (cla). **30-31 Alamy Images:** Stocktrek Images, Inc. / Andrew Chittock (c). **30 NAVY.mil:** U.S. Navy photo by Mass Communication Specialist 1st Class Brian Morales (bl). **31 NAVY.mil:** U.S. Navy photo by Mass Communication Specialist 2nd Class Betsy Knapper (tc). **Rex Shutterstock:** Terry Harris (cb). **32 Solar Impulse:** Revillard / Rezo.ch (c). **32-33 Solar Impulse:** Revillard / Rezo.ch (c). **33 Solar Impulse:** Revillard / Rezo.ch (t, br). **34 Columbia Helicopters:** (tl). **36 NASA:** (tc). **36-37 Corbis:** Peter Turnley (c). **NASA:** (b). **37 NAVY.mil:** U.S. Navy photo by Journalist 2nd Class Mark O'Donald (crb). **38 Edwards Airforce Base:** (bl). **42-43 Alamy Images:** age fotostock (t). **42 Getty Images:** USAF / Handout (bl). **43 Corbis:** Transtock / Robert Kerian (c). **U.S. Air Force:** Senior Master Sgt. Kim Frey (cra). **44 Alamy Images:** Stocktrek Images, Inc. (bl). **SpaceX:** (tr). **44-45 SpaceX:** (c). **45 SpaceX:** (tr). **46 Dreamstime.com:** Stepan Popov (cl). **NASA:** X-43A Development Team, DFRC, NASA (tr). **46-47 Dreamstime.com:** Ivan Cholakov (b). **47 Courtesy AgustaWestland:** (cr). **iStockphoto.com:** Ryan Mulhall (t). **NASA:** (cla). All other images © Dorling Kindersley. For further information see: www.dkimages.com

Contents

The first aeroplane

The American brothers Orville and Wilbur Wright launched the world's first powered aeroplane flight on 17 December 1903. Their longest flight that day lasted only 59 seconds, but it proved that powered flight was possible. Every aeroplane made since then has descended from the Wright Flyer.

The Wright Flyer

The Wright brothers built the Flyer in their workshop at Dayton, Ohio, USA. Starting from scratch, they designed and tested every part, from the propellers to the control system and wing shape. By 1905, a version of their Flyer could stay airborne for 38 minutes.

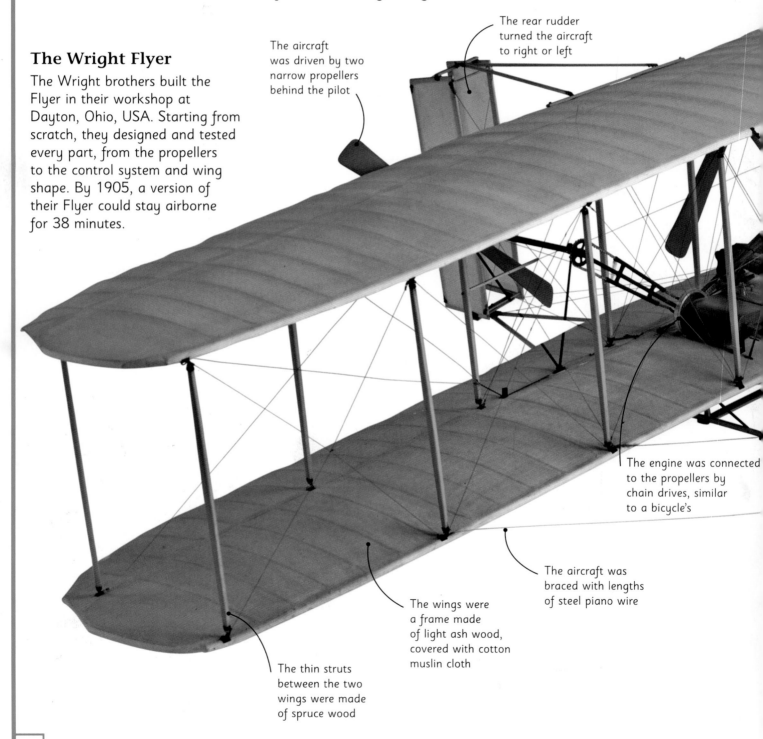

The aircraft was driven by two narrow propellers behind the pilot

The rear rudder turned the aircraft to right or left

The engine was connected to the propellers by chain drives, similar to a bicycle's

The aircraft was braced with lengths of steel piano wire

The wings were a frame made of light ash wood, covered with cotton muslin cloth

The thin struts between the two wings were made of spruce wood

The Flyer had a wingspan of around 12 m (40 ft)

In 1904, the Wright brothers' second plane, Flyer II, flew using a catapult

The aircraft sat on a launch rail

The catapult pushed the aircraft forwards by dropping a weight hung from a wooden frame

Launchpad

To help their aircraft take off without a strong wind, the Wright brothers designed a catapult in 1904. They made hundreds of flights using the catapult near their home in Ohio.

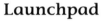

The elevators at the front of the aircraft could be moved to make it go up or down

The engine, made mostly of aluminium, weighed only 82 kg (180 lbs)

The pilot flew the plane lying on his front in a cradle on the lower wing, next to the engine

The engine had four cylinders, delivering 12 horsepower

Original engine

Charlie Taylor, an assistant to the Wright brothers, designed and built a petrol engine for the Flyer. It was about as powerful as the engines commonly used in modern-day go-karts for children.

This historic photo shows the very first aeroplane flight in 1903. Wilbur is standing on the right, while Orville lies inside, piloting the aircraft.

Gee Bee

Take a massive engine, add a pair of unusually short wings, and allow a tiny space for the pilot's cockpit. The result will probably look something like the spectacular Gee Bee Super Sportster, a plane that thrilled air-racing crowds in 1930s USA with its extraordinary speed and daredevil tactics.

This Gee Bee has reached a top speed of 305 kph (190 mph).

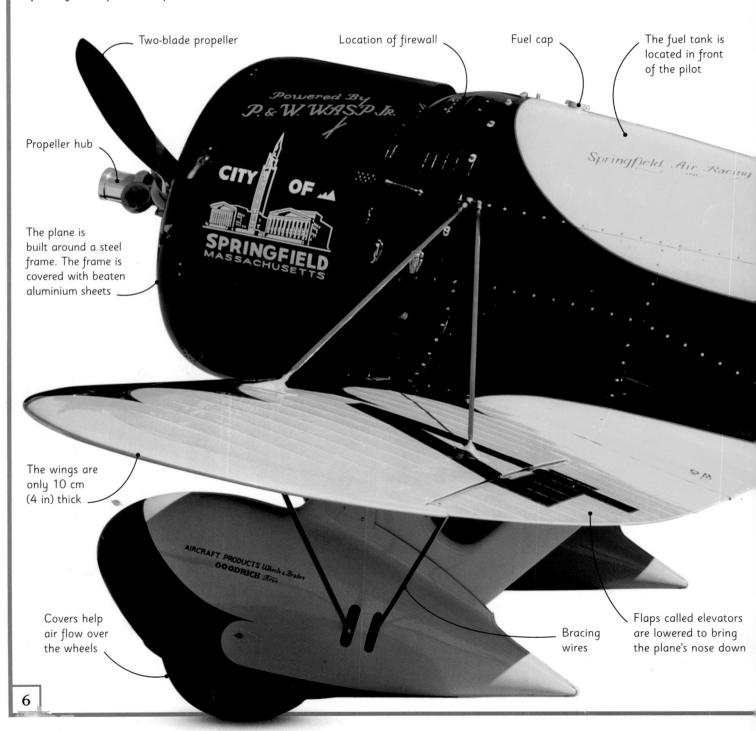

Two-blade propeller

Location of firewall

Fuel cap

The fuel tank is located in front of the pilot

Propeller hub

The plane is built around a steel frame. The frame is covered with beaten aluminium sheets

Powered By
P. & W. WASP Jr.

CITY OF
SPRINGFIELD
MASSACHUSETTS

Springfield Air Racing INC

The wings are only 10 cm (4 in) thick

AIRCRAFT PRODUCTS Wheels & Brakes
GOODRICH Tires

Covers help air flow over the wheels

Bracing wires

Flaps called elevators are lowered to bring the plane's nose down

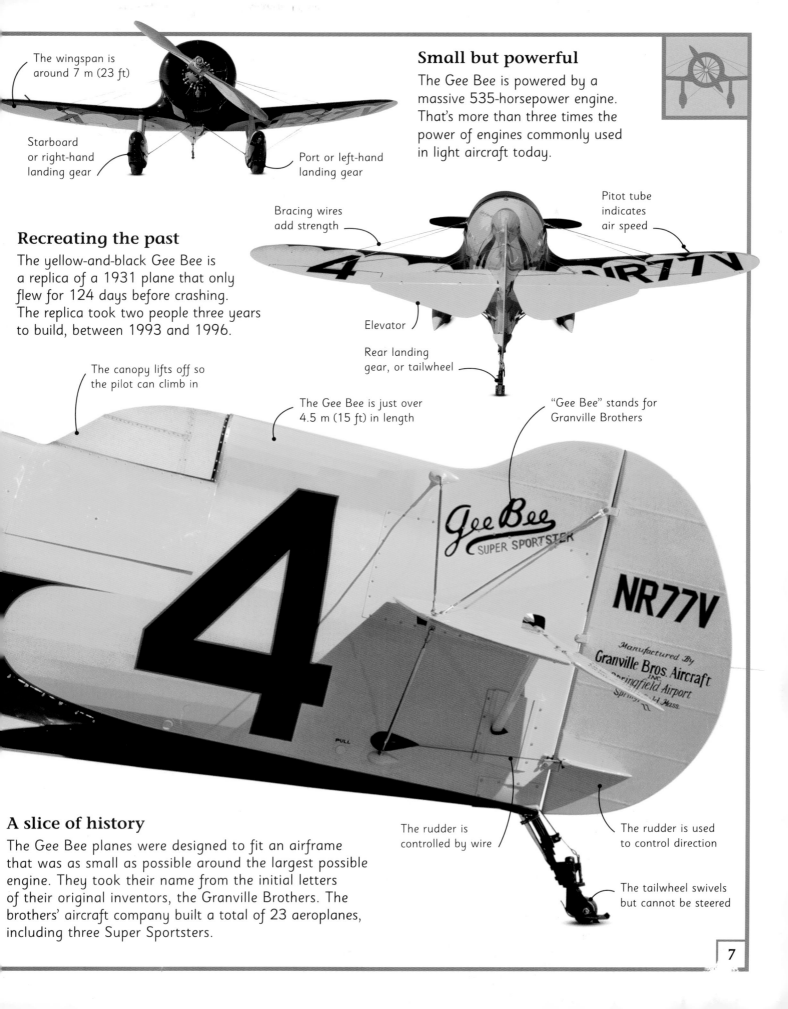

The wingspan is around 7 m (23 ft)

Starboard or right-hand landing gear

Port or left-hand landing gear

Small but powerful

The Gee Bee is powered by a massive 535-horsepower engine. That's more than three times the power of engines commonly used in light aircraft today.

Recreating the past

The yellow-and-black Gee Bee is a replica of a 1931 plane that only flew for 124 days before crashing. The replica took two people three years to build, between 1993 and 1996.

Bracing wires add strength

Pitot tube indicates air speed

Elevator

Rear landing gear, or tailwheel

The canopy lifts off so the pilot can climb in

The Gee Bee is just over 4.5 m (15 ft) in length

"Gee Bee" stands for Granville Brothers

Gee Bee
SUPER SPORTSTER

NR77V

Manufactured By
Granville Bros. Aircraft
INC.
Springfield Airport
Springfield Mass.

A slice of history

The Gee Bee planes were designed to fit an airframe that was as small as possible around the largest possible engine. They took their name from the initial letters of their original inventors, the Granville Brothers. The brothers' aircraft company built a total of 23 aeroplanes, including three Super Sportsters.

The rudder is controlled by wire

The rudder is used to control direction

The tailwheel swivels but cannot be steered

Experimental planes

In the 1940s, the speed of sound was seen as a huge invisible barrier to the speed at which an aeroplane could fly. Planes that flew too near to this speed broke up after terrible buffeting. This changed with the X-planes, an experimental series of aircraft built to break all previous speed and altitude records.

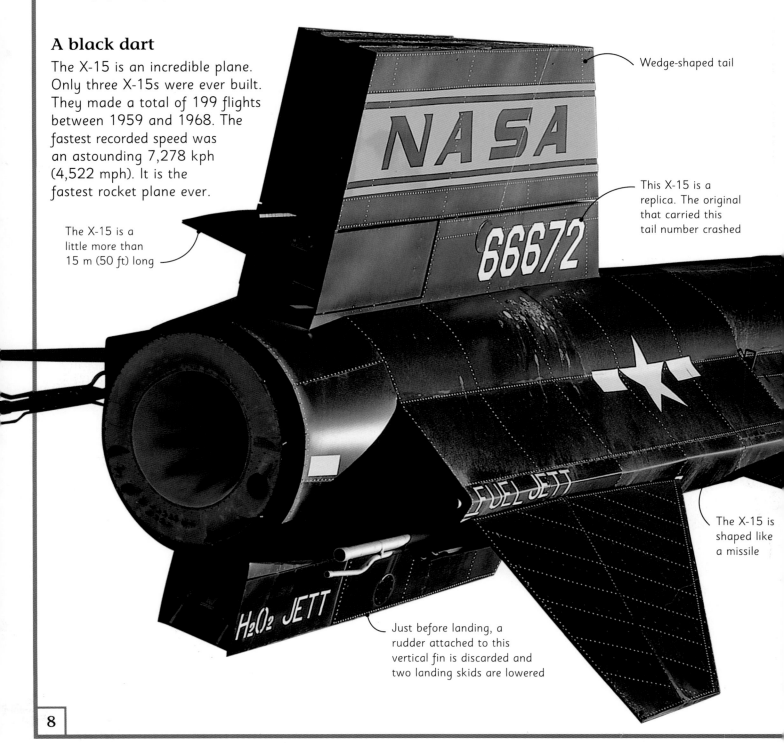

The X-1E and X-15 were launched from the wing of a larger plane.

A black dart

The X-15 is an incredible plane. Only three X-15s were ever built. They made a total of 199 flights between 1959 and 1968. The fastest recorded speed was an astounding 7,278 kph (4,522 mph). It is the fastest rocket plane ever.

The X-15 is a little more than 15 m (50 ft) long

Wedge-shaped tail

This X-15 is a replica. The original that carried this tail number crashed

The X-15 is shaped like a missile

Just before landing, a rudder attached to this vertical fin is discarded and two landing skids are lowered

Faster than a bullet?

This plane, the X-1E, is an adapted version of the X-1, the first plane to break the sound barrier. The X-1 planes were deliberately shaped to resemble bullets. As the X-1, this plane first flew in 1946; it was modified and renamed the X-1E in 1955.

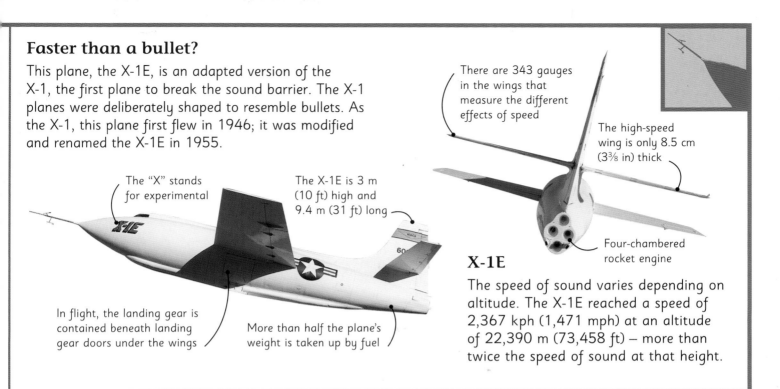

The "X" stands for experimental

The X-1E is 3 m (10 ft) high and 9.4 m (31 ft) long

In flight, the landing gear is contained beneath landing gear doors under the wings

More than half the plane's weight is taken up by fuel

There are 343 gauges in the wings that measure the different effects of speed

The high-speed wing is only 8.5 cm (3⅜ in) thick

Four-chambered rocket engine

X-1E

The speed of sound varies depending on altitude. The X-1E reached a speed of 2,367 kph (1,471 mph) at an altitude of 22,390 m (73,458 ft) – more than twice the speed of sound at that height.

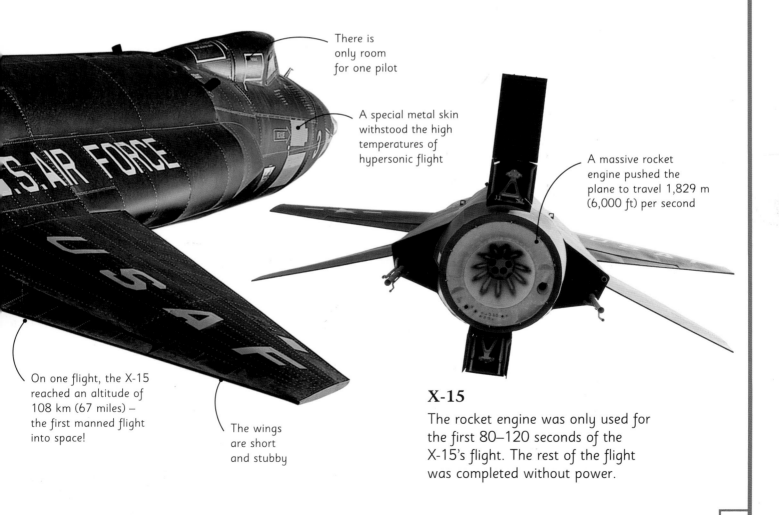

There is only room for one pilot

A special metal skin withstood the high temperatures of hypersonic flight

A massive rocket engine pushed the plane to travel 1,829 m (6,000 ft) per second

On one flight, the X-15 reached an altitude of 108 km (67 miles) – the first manned flight into space!

The wings are short and stubby

X-15

The rocket engine was only used for the first 80–120 seconds of the X-15's flight. The rest of the flight was completed without power.

Jumbo jet

The Boeing 747, also known as the jumbo jet, was the first wide-bodied aircraft ever produced. After its introduction in 1970, it doubled the number of passengers that could be taken on one aeroplane. Most jumbos seat 420 passengers, but some have an internal layout that allows them to carry 660 passengers!

Multi-purpose plane

The jumbo jet has been modified to perform a number of different tasks. Earlier, two jumbos were adapted to ferry the American space shuttle to and from its launch site. They were strengthened to have large struts to support the shuttle.

Talking big

The jumbo jet has a massive wingspan – more than 60 m (196 ft) wide. It has a wide body with space for two aisles. The passengers may be on board for 11 hours, so the plane will be loaded with more than 800 meals and about 120 litres (30 gallons) of juice and water. Everything about the plane is big!

The tailfin is 19.4 m (64 ft) high; as high as a six-storey building

Just like a car, a plane needs windscreen wipers

A wing's upper surface is curved more than its lower surface. As the engines push the plane forward, air rushing over the wings creates lift

The nose contains radar, which warns of obstacles around the aircraft – such as other planes, or an approaching storm

Each engine is covered with a protective cowling

An adult could stand up in each engine's air intake

A jumbo jet's landing gear is tested to support double the weight of the jet

The nose landing gear weighs more than a family-sized car

Upper passenger deck

Rudder

Passenger door

Baggage holds are located in the bottom of the fuselage

Going the distance

A jumbo jet can travel a third of the way around the world without having to stop and refuel. It carries more than 200,000 litres (54,000 gallons) of fuel in seven tanks – three located in each wing and one in the centre section.

A small engine in the tail powers the jumbo's electrical and air-conditioning systems when on the ground

Toilet waste is stored in large tanks in the belly of the fuselage

There are a total of 18 wheels, each 1.25 m (4 ft) in diameter

Exterior paint adds about 270 kg (595 lbs) to the weight of a jumbo jet

From bolts to wheels, there are about six million parts in a jumbo jet

Tailplane

The pilot and co-pilot sit on the flight deck surrounded by controls. There are even switches above their heads.

The fuselage wall is 19 cm (7½ in) thick and includes a layer of sound and heat insulation

Fuel is carried in the wings and in a centre section between the wings

Landing light

The four engines are attached to the lower side of the wings

A fan draws air into each turbofan engine

Each of the four main landing gear mechanisms, or bogies, has four wheels

Biplane

In the early years of flight, most aircraft were biplanes – they had two wings, one above the other. Biplanes could not fly as fast as single-wing aeroplanes but they were popular among pilots because they were sturdy and reliable. The Boeing Stearman was one of the most popular biplanes, and is sometimes flown even today.

During World War II, most US military pilots learned to fly in the Stearman Model 75 aircraft.

Training plane

The Boeing Stearman Model 75 was first flown in 1934. It was primarily used as a training aircraft, but it was also popular with farmers for spraying crops and with stunt fliers performing aerobatic displays at air shows.

The Stearman was very stable, and ideal for flying-show stunts such as wing walking.

The propeller drove the plane forwards at a maximum speed of 217 kph (135 mph)

The air-cooled radial engine delivered around 220 horsepower

Each wheel was attached to a single metal leg

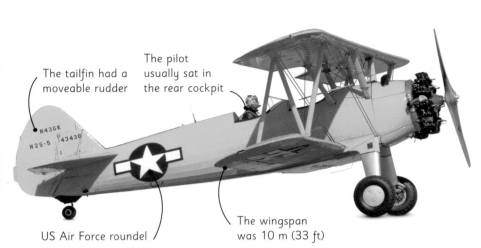

The tailfin had a moveable rudder

The pilot usually sat in the rear cockpit

US Air Force roundel

The wingspan was 10 m (33 ft)

Going strong

The Boeing Stearman Model 75 was a sturdy aeroplane that allowed even an inexperienced pilot to fly safely. Around 8,500 Stearmans were built in the 1930s and 1940s, making it the most produced US single-engine biplane in history.

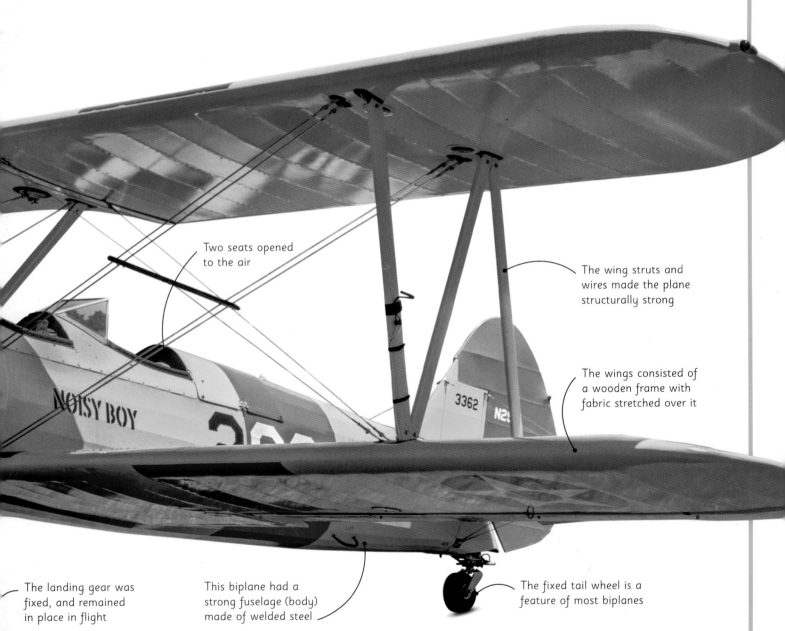

Two seats opened to the air

The wing struts and wires made the plane structurally strong

The wings consisted of a wooden frame with fabric stretched over it

The landing gear was fixed, and remained in place in flight

This biplane had a strong fuselage (body) made of welded steel

The fixed tail wheel is a feature of most biplanes

Agricultural aeroplane

Some farmers spray their crops to prevent damage from pests or to fertilize the crops to help them grow. They may be growing corn, peanuts, or cotton. Using an aeroplane is faster than using a tractor – a plane will swoop low over a field and spray a crop in minutes.

The white tip makes a white ring when the propeller spins, making it easier to see

The plane's single 750-horsepower engine is located behind the propeller

Engine exhaust

An unusual feature of this plane is that the propeller can be used to reverse the plane while taxiing on the ground

The propeller makes 2,000 revolutions (turns) each minute

Each wing is almost 2 m (6 ft) wide

Fuel is carried in the wings

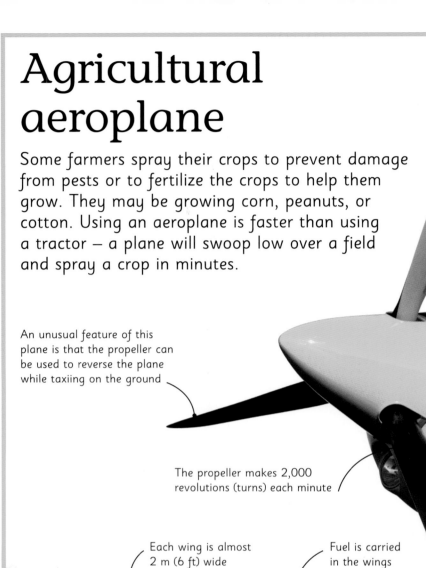

Air leaving the wings creates a downwash that forces the spray to cover both the top and the bottom of the crop's leaves.

Metal struts, known as boom hangars, support the spray boom

Air intake for engine

The pump that feeds the liquid product to the boom is turned by air flowing into this propeller

The landing gear is fixed and doesn't retract during flight

Loading up

The hopper is usually filled with dry material from the top, or liquid material through the bottom loading valve to which a large hose will be attached. It takes just three minutes to load 2,270 litres (500 gallons) of liquid. The plane can usually fly for about 2½ hours without refuelling.

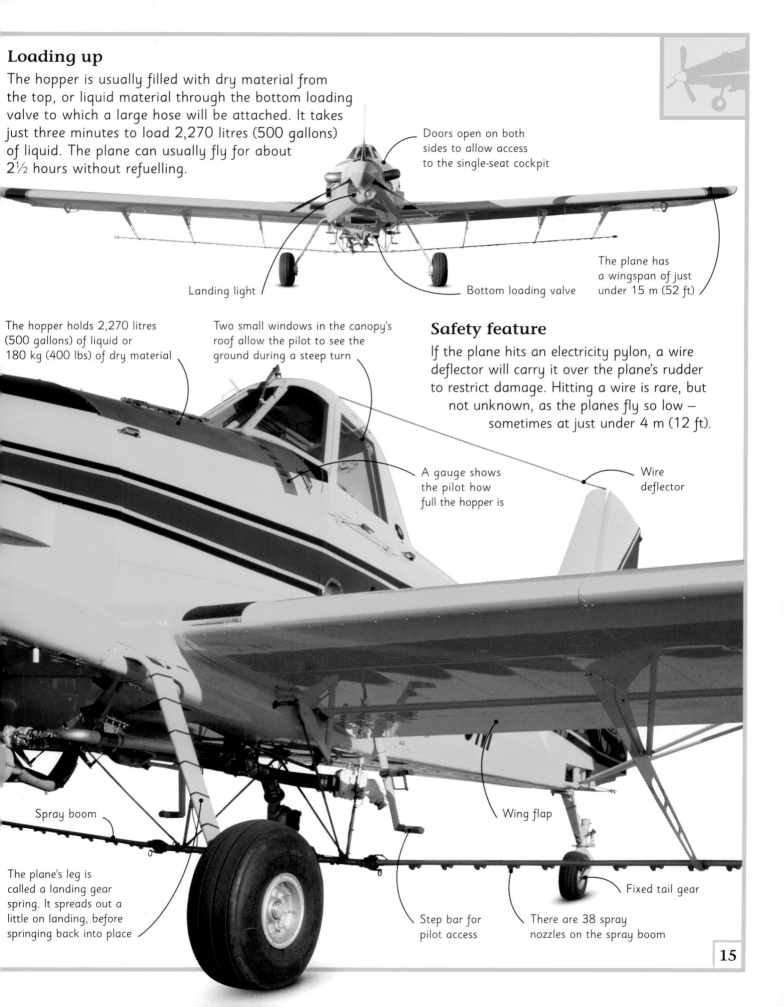

Doors open on both sides to allow access to the single-seat cockpit

Landing light

Bottom loading valve

The plane has a wingspan of just under 15 m (52 ft)

The hopper holds 2,270 litres (500 gallons) of liquid or 180 kg (400 lbs) of dry material

Two small windows in the canopy's roof allow the pilot to see the ground during a steep turn

Safety feature

If the plane hits an electricity pylon, a wire deflector will carry it over the plane's rudder to restrict damage. Hitting a wire is rare, but not unknown, as the planes fly so low – sometimes at just under 4 m (12 ft).

A gauge shows the pilot how full the hopper is

Wire deflector

Spray boom

Wing flap

The plane's leg is called a landing gear spring. It spreads out a little on landing, before springing back into place

Step bar for pilot access

There are 38 spray nozzles on the spray boom

Fixed tail gear

Kit aeroplane

Imagine buying a kit and building your own aeroplane in a large garage! You could put together a plane like the Velocity, an eye-catching four-seater that looks very different to most light aircraft in the skies today.

The winglet helps lift the aircraft and acts as a vertical stabilizer

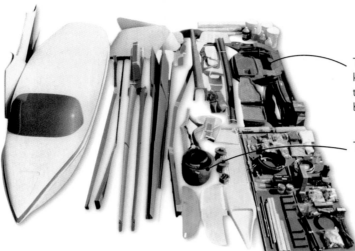

The build-a-plane kits come with all the necessary nuts, bolts, and screws

Tyres

The single gull-wing door opens upwards

The plane seats four people, including the pilot. It can carry 272 kg (600 lbs) in weight of passengers and luggage

One big jigsaw puzzle

This Velocity kit takes about 1,200 hours to build. That's the same as working a five-day week for 34 weeks.

VELOCI

Pitot tube

The fibreglass body is so light that an adult can lift the nose off the ground

Small wings at the front, called canards, help to lift the aircraft

Step to aid access to cabin

In flight, the Velocity can cruise along at about 320 kph (200 mph)

Nosewheel

Why is it white?

Under the fibreglass surface is a lightweight core material that shrinks in excessive heat. A white surface doesn't absorb as much heat as a dark surface, which means that the core material is not as likely to get so hot that it shrinks.

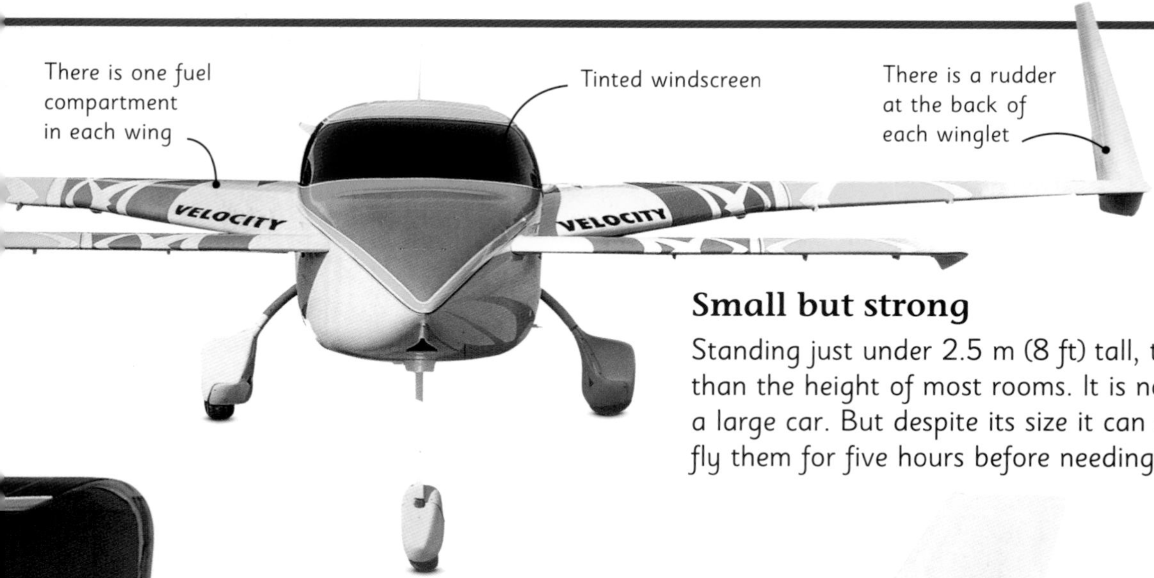

There is one fuel compartment in each wing

Tinted windscreen

There is a rudder at the back of each winglet

Small but strong

Standing just under 2.5 m (8 ft) tall, the aircraft is shorter than the height of most rooms. It is not much longer than a large car. But despite its size it can seat four people and fly them for five hours before needing to stop and refuel.

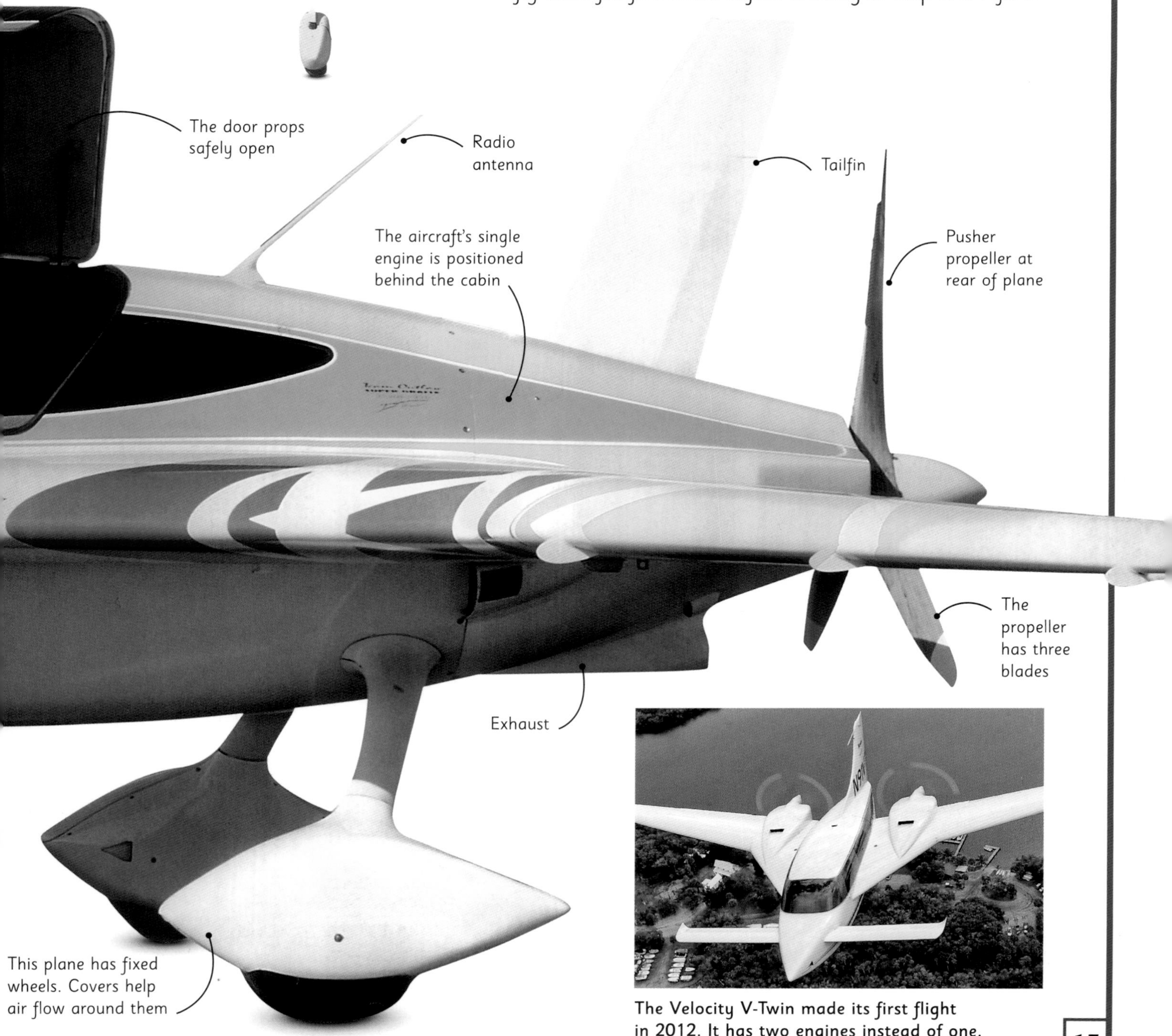

The door props safely open

Radio antenna

Tailfin

The aircraft's single engine is positioned behind the cabin

Pusher propeller at rear of plane

Exhaust

The propeller has three blades

This plane has fixed wheels. Covers help air flow around them

The Velocity V-Twin made its first flight in 2012. It has two engines instead of one.

Stunt planes

Go to an air show and you'll see brightly coloured planes zipping past, wingtips almost touching. Watch as highly trained pilots take the planes into intricate loops, rolls, and flips. It's an exciting sight, with the stunt planes performing incredible air acrobatics.

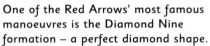

One of the Red Arrows' most famous manoeuvres is the Diamond Nine formation – a perfect diamond shape.

Who are they?

The red, white, and blue colours of these planes identify them as the display team of the Royal Air Force Red Arrows, based in England. The team have taken part in air shows all around the world.

Single tailfin

One of two semicircular air intakes

The plane's wingspan is 9 m (31 ft)

Flaps help to control an aeroplane during takeoff or landing

The planes are capable of reaching speeds of more than 1,000 kph (620 mph)

The rudder is used to control direction

The plane is 12 m (39 ft) in length

X294

Jet exhaust

A wing fence improves the flow of air over the wing

The front of an aeroplane's wing is known as the leading edge. The back is the trailing edge

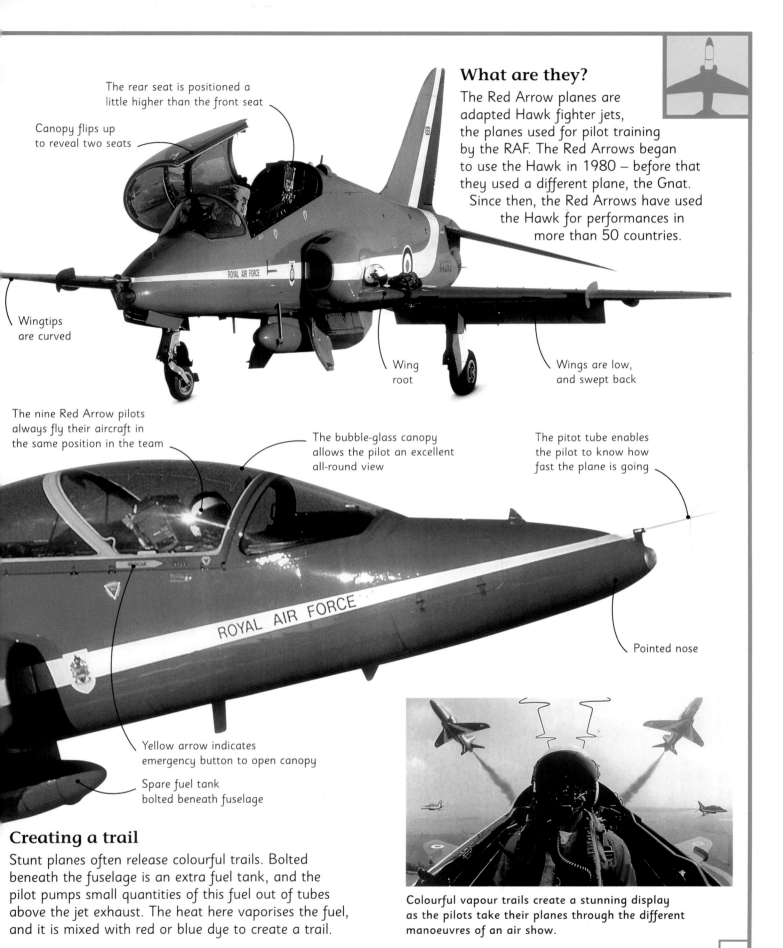

The rear seat is positioned a little higher than the front seat

Canopy flips up to reveal two seats

Wingtips are curved

Wing root

Wings are low, and swept back

What are they?

The Red Arrow planes are adapted Hawk fighter jets, the planes used for pilot training by the RAF. The Red Arrows began to use the Hawk in 1980 – before that they used a different plane, the Gnat. Since then, the Red Arrows have used the Hawk for performances in more than 50 countries.

The nine Red Arrow pilots always fly their aircraft in the same position in the team

The bubble-glass canopy allows the pilot an excellent all-round view

The pitot tube enables the pilot to know how fast the plane is going

Pointed nose

ROYAL AIR FORCE

Yellow arrow indicates emergency button to open canopy

Spare fuel tank bolted beneath fuselage

Creating a trail

Stunt planes often release colourful trails. Bolted beneath the fuselage is an extra fuel tank, and the pilot pumps small quantities of this fuel out of tubes above the jet exhaust. The heat here vaporises the fuel, and it is mixed with red or blue dye to create a trail.

Colourful vapour trails create a stunning display as the pilots take their planes through the different manoeuvres of an air show.

Flying laboratory

The ER-2 has four compartments that hold experiments. One is in the fuselage, one is in the nose, and two are in pods that can be attached to the wings.

This unusual-looking, long-nosed plane is designed to cruise at altitudes of around 22 km (13.5 miles). That's more than twice the cruising altitude of a jumbo jet! It needs to do this because it is a flying science aircraft, or flying laboratory, specially equipped to collect information about the Earth. Its official name is the ER-2.

A typical mission

Following takeoff, the ER-2 will reach its cruising altitude in around 20 minutes. The plane can travel more than 4,800 km (3,000 miles) each time it goes on a mission, though typical missions are shorter. It will usually be up for around six hours.

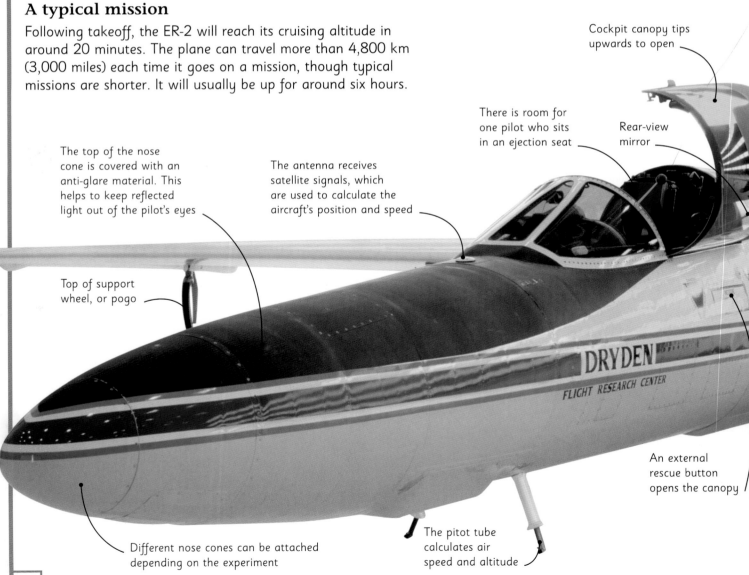

Cockpit canopy tips upwards to open

There is room for one pilot who sits in an ejection seat

Rear-view mirror

The top of the nose cone is covered with an anti-glare material. This helps to keep reflected light out of the pilot's eyes

The antenna receives satellite signals, which are used to calculate the aircraft's position and speed

Top of support wheel, or pogo

DRYDEN
FLIGHT RESEARCH CENTER

An external rescue button opens the canopy

Different nose cones can be attached depending on the experiment

The pitot tube calculates air speed and altitude

What does it do?

The ER-2 monitors changes in the weather, the sea, and geography of the Earth. It can be used to test the behaviour of new technology under extreme conditions.

The ER-2 is operated by NASA (National Aeronautics and Space Administration)

Most fuel is carried in the wings

An equipment bay is located just behind the cockpit

Location of engine

Small wheels, known as pogos, support the wings on the ground. The pogos fall away on takeoff

Six probes collect high-altitude particles for analysis

There is a rudder on the tailfin

VHF radio antenna

There are two red anti-collision lights on the top of the fuselage

In flight, the ER-2's cockpit is pressurized. The pilot also wears a pressure suit for extra protection.

Tailplane

80-1063

Aircraft registration numbers on open speed brake

The wingspan is an incredible 31.5 m (104 ft), which is about 12 m (40 ft) more than the plane's length

Main landing gear

This experimental pod is used to collect particles or cosmic dust at high altitudes

Chocks are left under the wheels when the aircraft is stationary

Spitfire

The British Supermarine Spitfire is known for having successfully fought the German Luftwaffe air force in the Battle of Britain during World War II. One of the fastest propeller-driven aeroplanes ever built, it was a highly effective and reliable war machine.

The Spitfire was one of the most easily recognizable aircraft ever built because of the distinctive curved shape of its wings.

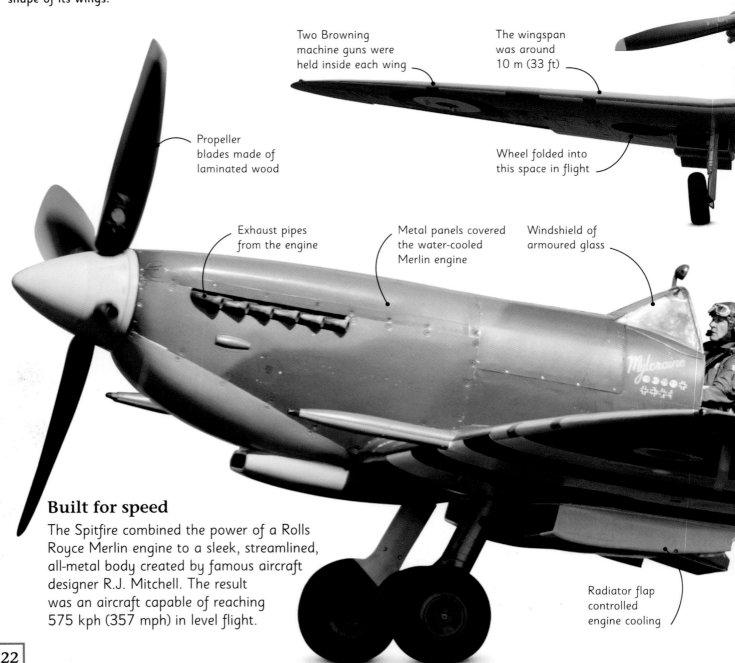

Two Browning machine guns were held inside each wing

The wingspan was around 10 m (33 ft)

Propeller blades made of laminated wood

Wheel folded into this space in flight

Exhaust pipes from the engine

Metal panels covered the water-cooled Merlin engine

Windshield of armoured glass

Radiator flap controlled engine cooling

Built for speed

The Spitfire combined the power of a Rolls Royce Merlin engine to a sleek, streamlined, all-metal body created by famous aircraft designer R.J. Mitchell. The result was an aircraft capable of reaching 575 kph (357 mph) in level flight.

Versatile plane

First introduced in 1938, the Spitfire remained in service until the 1950s. In total, 24 different versions of the Spitfire were built, with small changes made to the wings, engine, and weapons.

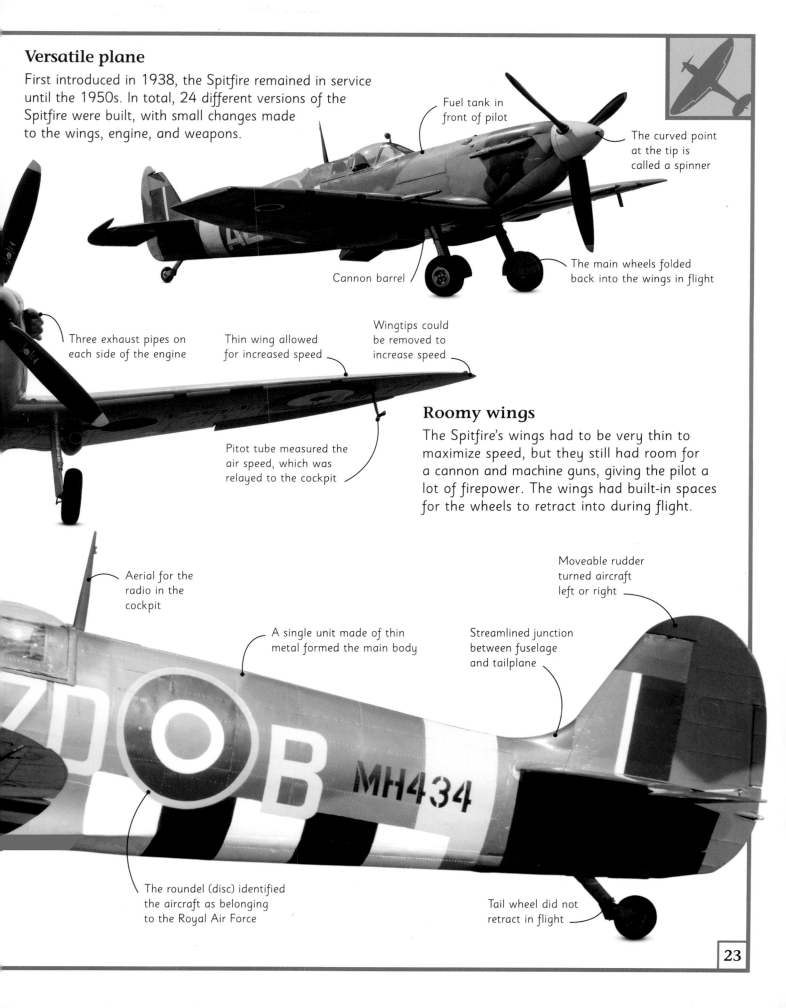

Fuel tank in front of pilot

The curved point at the tip is called a spinner

The main wheels folded back into the wings in flight

Cannon barrel

Three exhaust pipes on each side of the engine

Thin wing allowed for increased speed

Wingtips could be removed to increase speed

Pitot tube measured the air speed, which was relayed to the cockpit

Roomy wings

The Spitfire's wings had to be very thin to maximize speed, but they still had room for a cannon and machine guns, giving the pilot a lot of firepower. The wings had built-in spaces for the wheels to retract into during flight.

Aerial for the radio in the cockpit

A single unit made of thin metal formed the main body

Moveable rudder turned aircraft left or right

Streamlined junction between fuselage and tailplane

MH434

The roundel (disc) identified the aircraft as belonging to the Royal Air Force

Tail wheel did not retract in flight

Microlight

Although it looks small, this microlight can stay in the air for up to four hours, burning up fuel at the rate of 12 litres (3 gallons) per hour. Many microlight pilots take part in competitions, carrying out a series of tasks such as photographing things on the ground, or switching off the engine before landing. It is an exciting sport.

Microlights usually fly at about 900 m (3,000 ft) – a jumbo jet flies at 10 times that height.

This zip is opened during the preflight inspection to allow the pilot to check that the cables are correctly connected

Battens hold the wing material taut

Rigging lines strengthen the microlight

A safe flight

Before a microlight pilot can take off, he or she will check over the aircraft, just like a pilot does for a larger plane. The pilot walks around the microlight, checking that the controls are rigged correctly, the wing is properly secured to the body, the tyres are okay, and also testing the engine and the exhaust. This can take about 20 minutes.

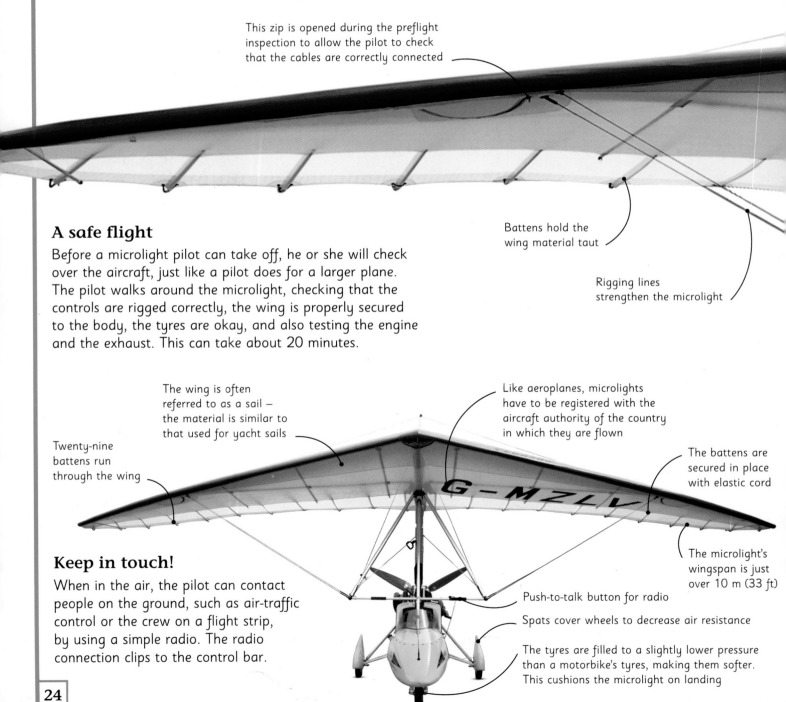

The wing is often referred to as a sail – the material is similar to that used for yacht sails

Twenty-nine battens run through the wing

Like aeroplanes, microlights have to be registered with the aircraft authority of the country in which they are flown

The battens are secured in place with elastic cord

The microlight's wingspan is just over 10 m (33 ft)

Keep in touch!

When in the air, the pilot can contact people on the ground, such as air-traffic control or the crew on a flight strip, by using a simple radio. The radio connection clips to the control bar.

Push-to-talk button for radio

Spats cover wheels to decrease air resistance

The tyres are filled to a slightly lower pressure than a motorbike's tyres, making them softer. This cushions the microlight on landing

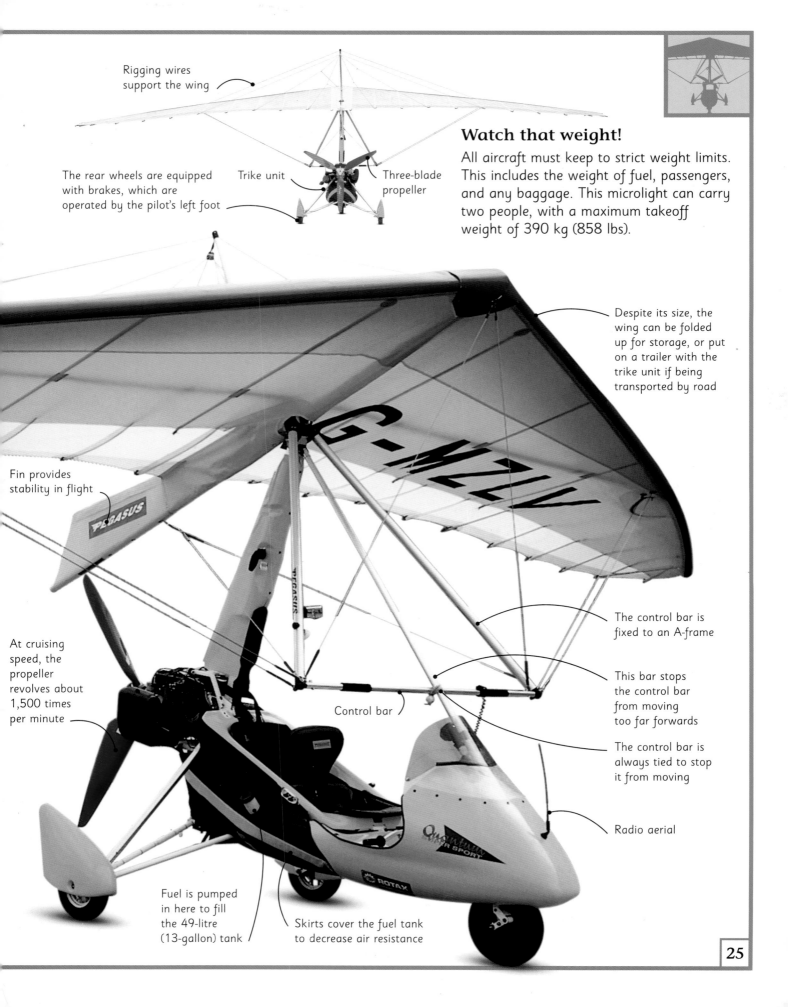

Rigging wires support the wing

The rear wheels are equipped with brakes, which are operated by the pilot's left foot

Trike unit

Three-blade propeller

Watch that weight!

All aircraft must keep to strict weight limits. This includes the weight of fuel, passengers, and any baggage. This microlight can carry two people, with a maximum takeoff weight of 390 kg (858 lbs).

Despite its size, the wing can be folded up for storage, or put on a trailer with the trike unit if being transported by road

Fin provides stability in flight

At cruising speed, the propeller revolves about 1,500 times per minute

Control bar

The control bar is fixed to an A-frame

This bar stops the control bar from moving too far forwards

The control bar is always tied to stop it from moving

Radio aerial

Fuel is pumped in here to fill the 49-litre (13-gallon) tank

Skirts cover the fuel tank to decrease air resistance

Concorde

Concorde was a supersonic airliner, capable of carrying passengers at more than twice the speed of sound. In a record flight, it crossed the Atlantic Ocean, from New York to London, in just under three hours — less than half the time a jumbo jet takes. It also cruised along at about twice the altitude of a jumbo, so its passengers could see the curve of the Earth. Concorde was in regular service with British and French airlines from 1976 to 2003.

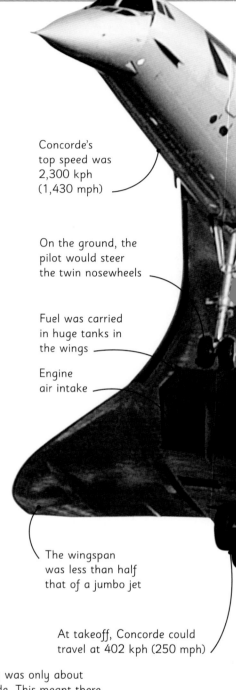

Concorde's top speed was 2,300 kph (1,430 mph)

On the ground, the pilot would steer the twin nosewheels

Fuel was carried in huge tanks in the wings

Engine air intake

The wingspan was less than half that of a jumbo jet

At takeoff, Concorde could travel at 402 kph (250 mph)

Once in the air, Concorde guzzled fuel at the rate of 427 litres (111 gallons) each minute. It could travel about 5,900 km (3,740 miles) without stopping to refuel, and flew at an altitude of about 16 km (10 miles), which is too high to be affected by air turbulence.

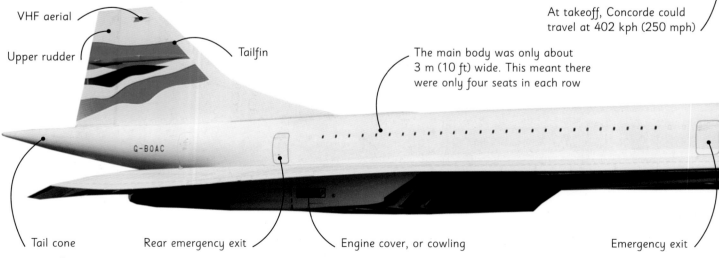

VHF aerial

Upper rudder

Tailfin

The main body was only about 3 m (10 ft) wide. This meant there were only four seats in each row

G-BOAC

Tail cone

Rear emergency exit

Engine cover, or cowling

Emergency exit

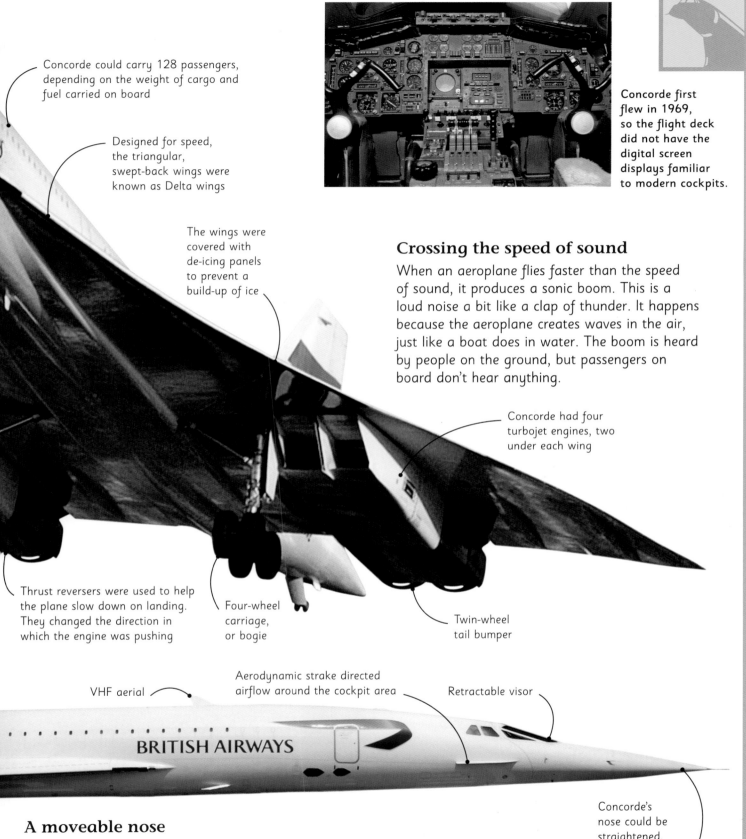

Concorde could carry 128 passengers, depending on the weight of cargo and fuel carried on board

Designed for speed, the triangular, swept-back wings were known as Delta wings

The wings were covered with de-icing panels to prevent a build-up of ice

Concorde first flew in 1969, so the flight deck did not have the digital screen displays familiar to modern cockpits.

Crossing the speed of sound

When an aeroplane flies faster than the speed of sound, it produces a sonic boom. This is a loud noise a bit like a clap of thunder. It happens because the aeroplane creates waves in the air, just like a boat does in water. The boom is heard by people on the ground, but passengers on board don't hear anything.

Concorde had four turbojet engines, two under each wing

Thrust reversers were used to help the plane slow down on landing. They changed the direction in which the engine was pushing

Four-wheel carriage, or bogie

Twin-wheel tail bumper

VHF aerial

Aerodynamic strake directed airflow around the cockpit area

Retractable visor

BRITISH AIRWAYS

Concorde's nose could be straightened, or dropped down

A moveable nose

Concorde's nose straightened out when the plane was flying. This helped the plane to cut through the air. It dropped down for takeoff and landing, so that the pilot had a better view of the runway. The nose contained radar equipment.

Blackbird

The Blackbird, or SR-71A, was the perfect spy plane. Not only could it fly at an amazing 3,218 kph (2,000 mph) – more than three times the speed of sound – but its onboard cameras could read a number plate on a car from 27 km (17 miles) up. The Blackbird served with the US Air Force from 1964 to 1998.

The plane expanded by 28 cm (11 in) in flight

Protective covers had to be removed before takeoff

Because the Blackbird flew so high and so fast, no enemy missiles or aircraft could catch it. Not a single Blackbird was ever shot down.

The SR-71A carried a crew of two – a pilot and a reconnaissance systems officer

In flight, the cone pulled back 66 cm (26 in) to control the air allowed into the engine

The whole rudder moved on a hinge at the base

The plane was refuelled in mid-air through a refuelling port or opening in the Blackbird's skin

A curved edge, known as a chine, provided lift and stability to the front of the aircraft

Circular air intake (protected when on the ground) supplied air to the engine

Fuel more than doubled the empty weight of the plane

Blackbird was faster than a rifle bullet

Landing lights

Front landing gear

Smash those records!

The Blackbird remains the fastest jet-engine aircraft ever built. It set a number of world speed records in 1976, reaching 3,530 kph (2,193 mph). It also set an altitude record for a jet-engine aircraft of 25,930 m (85,069 ft).

Don't touch!

By the time it landed, the Blackbird's body became too hot to touch for about an hour. The pilot had to step clear on special steps that were wheeled up to the plane. Parts of the plane's body reached the same temperature as that of a hot oven.

There were ejection seats in case of emergency

Red lines marked the limits of where ground mechanics could step

One of two engines

Food was carried in tubes. The crew held the tubes against the cockpit glass to warm the food!

Getting bigger

Each engine was almost 5.5 m (18 ft) in length. But it expanded another 15 cm (6 in) in flight because of the heat!

The crew had to wear protective, high altitude pressure suits, similar to the suits astronauts wear

In less than one hour, Blackbird could photograph an area of 259,000 sq km (100,000 sq miles)

One jet engine was contained here

Landing gear retracted when the plane was in flight to produce a smooth, aerodynamic shape

Gear doors closed to seal in the landing gear after takeoff

When the plane climbed, the engines used up a total of about 36,370 litres (8,000 gallons) of fuel per hour

Tyres were 10 times thicker than a car tyre

Jump jet

First flown in 1967, the Harrier jump jet was the world's first vertical, or short, takeoff and landing jet. Not only could it fly at over 960 kph (600 mph), it could also take off straight up from the ground without a runway, hover stationary in the air, and land in a space the size of a tennis court.

Pylon for carrying missiles or bombs

External fuel tank carried on underwing pylon

Pegasus turbofan engine

Forward-looking infrared (heat) sensor

Bubble cockpit canopy gives all-round vision

Technical wizardry

The secret of the Harrier's success lay in its Pegasus engine's four swivelling nozzles. By adjusting the angle of these nozzles, the pilot could direct the jet thrust straight to the rear of the aeroplane for ordinary flight or at various angles downward during landing and takeoff.

Nozzle swivels downwards for takeoff and landing

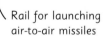

Rail for launching air-to-air missiles

Balancing act

Vertically taking off or landing the Harrier took a lot of skill. Extra control nozzles at the tail, wingtips, and nose helped balance the aircraft above the ground. For a pilot, it was like trying to stay upright on a stationary bicycle.

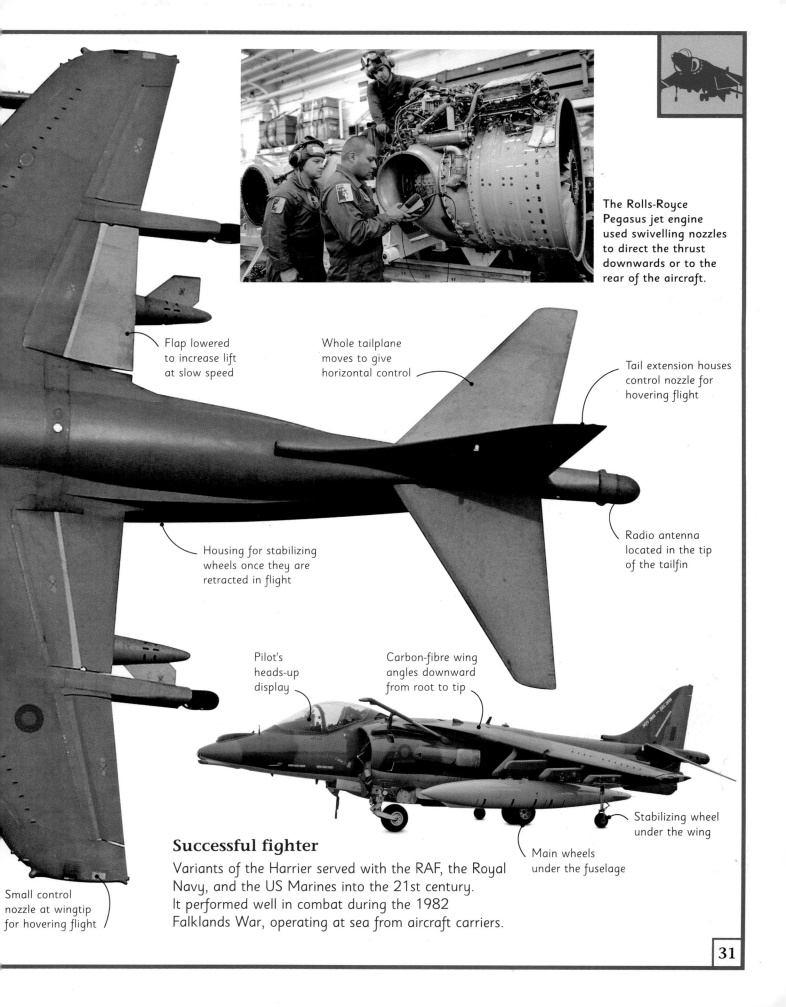

The Rolls-Royce Pegasus jet engine used swivelling nozzles to direct the thrust downwards or to the rear of the aircraft.

Flap lowered to increase lift at slow speed

Whole tailplane moves to give horizontal control

Tail extension houses control nozzle for hovering flight

Radio antenna located in the tip of the tailfin

Housing for stabilizing wheels once they are retracted in flight

Pilot's heads-up display

Carbon-fibre wing angles downward from root to tip

Stabilizing wheel under the wing

Main wheels under the fuselage

Small control nozzle at wingtip for hovering flight

Successful fighter

Variants of the Harrier served with the RAF, the Royal Navy, and the US Marines into the 21st century. It performed well in combat during the 1982 Falklands War, operating at sea from aircraft carriers.

Solar Impulse

Imagine an aircraft that flies without fuel, causing zero damage to the environment, and that can stay airborne more or less forever! In 2015, Solar Impulse 2 travelled 7,212 km (4,481 miles) from Japan to Hawaii. It flew for almost five days non-stop, and drew its energy only from the Sun's rays.

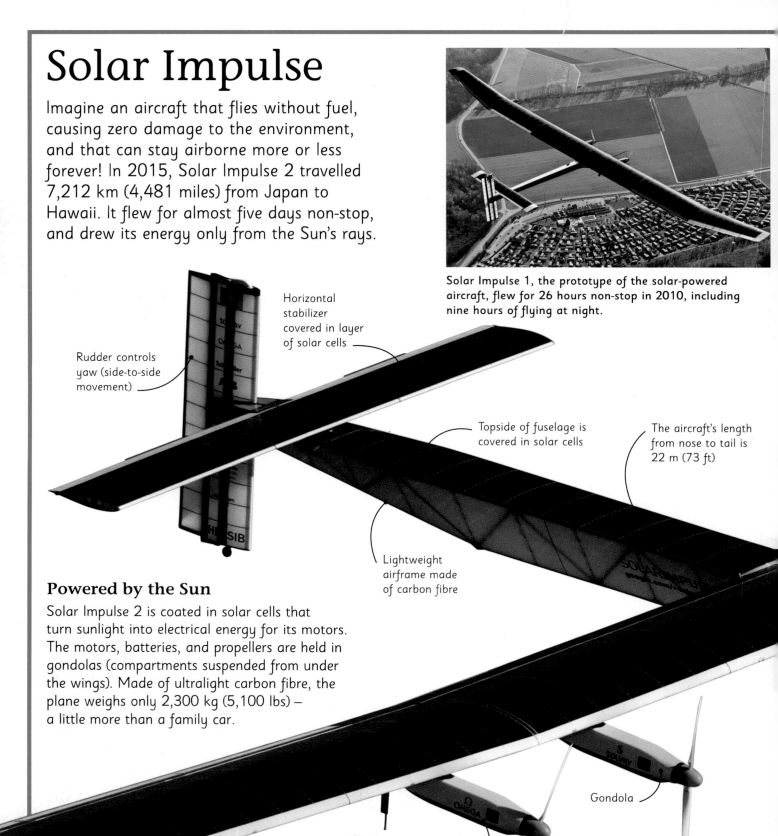

Solar Impulse 1, the prototype of the solar-powered aircraft, flew for 26 hours non-stop in 2010, including nine hours of flying at night.

Horizontal stabilizer covered in layer of solar cells

Rudder controls yaw (side-to-side movement)

Topside of fuselage is covered in solar cells

The aircraft's length from nose to tail is 22 m (73 ft)

Lightweight airframe made of carbon fibre

Powered by the Sun

Solar Impulse 2 is coated in solar cells that turn sunlight into electrical energy for its motors. The motors, batteries, and propellers are held in gondolas (compartments suspended from under the wings). Made of ultralight carbon fibre, the plane weighs only 2,300 kg (5,100 lbs) – a little more than a family car.

Gondola

These compartments hold rechargeable batteries that store power for night flying

The wingspan is 72 m (236 ft). That's bigger than a Boeing 747!

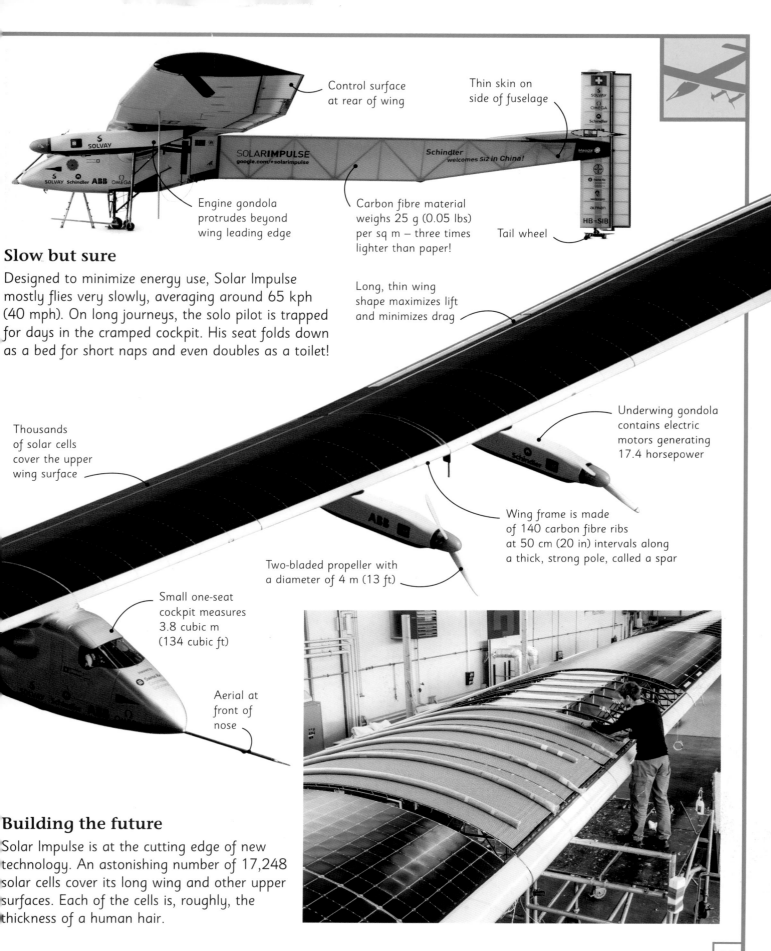

Control surface at rear of wing

Thin skin on side of fuselage

Engine gondola protrudes beyond wing leading edge

Carbon fibre material weighs 25 g (0.05 lbs) per sq m – three times lighter than paper!

Tail wheel

Slow but sure

Designed to minimize energy use, Solar Impulse mostly flies very slowly, averaging around 65 kph (40 mph). On long journeys, the solo pilot is trapped for days in the cramped cockpit. His seat folds down as a bed for short naps and even doubles as a toilet!

Long, thin wing shape maximizes lift and minimizes drag

Thousands of solar cells cover the upper wing surface

Underwing gondola contains electric motors generating 17.4 horsepower

Wing frame is made of 140 carbon fibre ribs at 50 cm (20 in) intervals along a thick, strong pole, called a spar

Two-bladed propeller with a diameter of 4 m (13 ft)

Small one-seat cockpit measures 3.8 cubic m (134 cubic ft)

Aerial at front of nose

Building the future

Solar Impulse is at the cutting edge of new technology. An astonishing number of 17,248 solar cells cover its long wing and other upper surfaces. Each of the cells is, roughly, the thickness of a human hair.

Chinook helicopter

A helicopter can hover and pick up a load from a very restricted space. It might be lifting logs from a heavily wooded hillside or transporting huge pipes. This Chinook helicopter is unusually powerful. It has been stripped of unnecessary equipment to make it lighter so that it can lift more than its own weight in cargo. It is known as a utility Chinook.

The hefty steel cable used to lift loads is 2.5 cm (1 in) thick and 60 m (200 ft) long.

A thirst for fuel

Helicopter engines burn up a lot of fuel spinning the rotors to lift the machine up. During routine heavy-lift operations, this Chinook uses 1,515 litres (333 gallons) of fuel per hour. It is typically refuelled every 1½ hours.

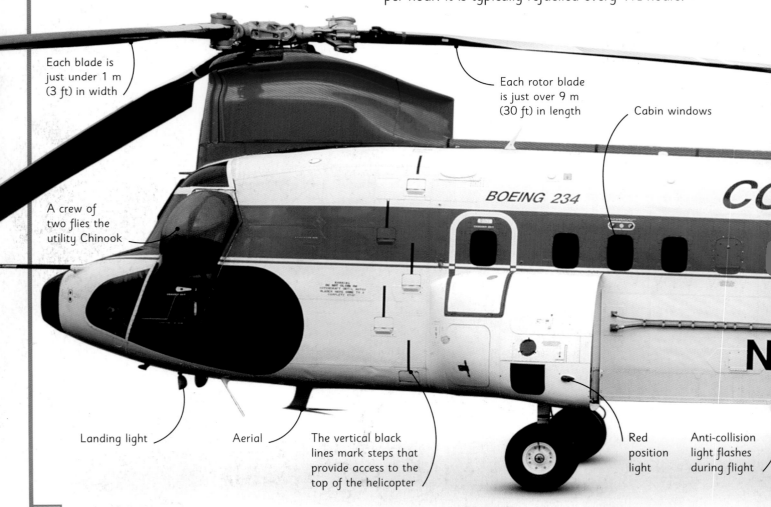

Each blade is just under 1 m (3 ft) in width

Each rotor blade is just over 9 m (30 ft) in length

Cabin windows

BOEING 234

A crew of two flies the utility Chinook

Landing light

Aerial

The vertical black lines mark steps that provide access to the top of the helicopter

Red position light

Anti-collision light flashes during flight

Flight control

A pilot works with a copilot, so the cockpit controls are the same on both sides. Both pilot and copilot have more than 150 control buttons and switches around them.

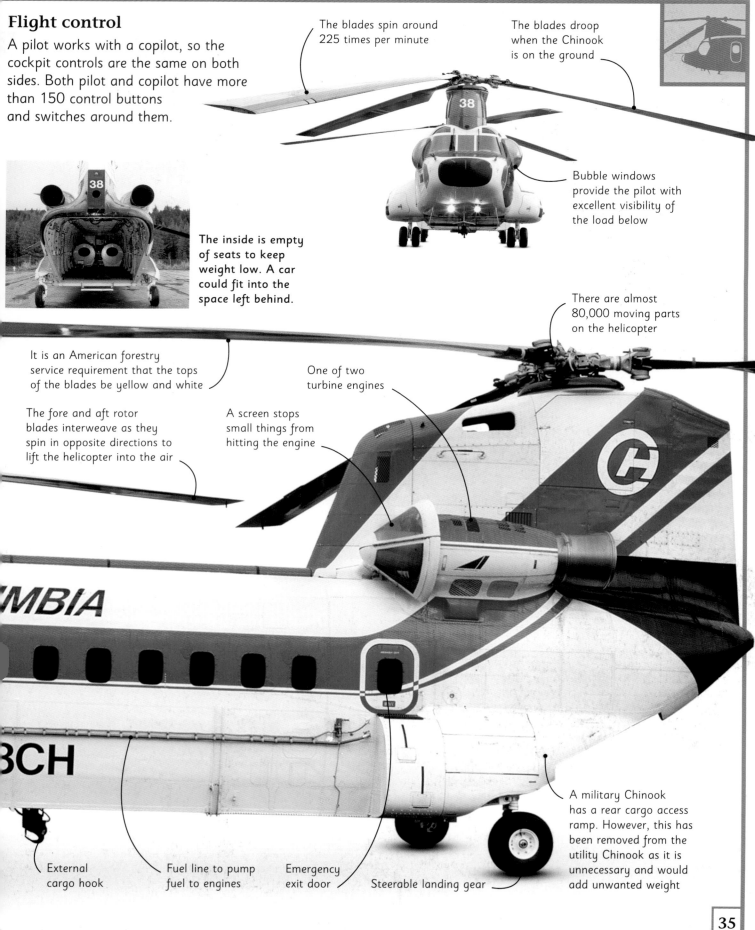

The blades spin around 225 times per minute

The blades droop when the Chinook is on the ground

Bubble windows provide the pilot with excellent visibility of the load below

The inside is empty of seats to keep weight low. A car could fit into the space left behind.

There are almost 80,000 moving parts on the helicopter

It is an American forestry service requirement that the tops of the blades be yellow and white

One of two turbine engines

The fore and aft rotor blades interweave as they spin in opposite directions to lift the helicopter into the air

A screen stops small things from hitting the engine

External cargo hook

Fuel line to pump fuel to engines

Emergency exit door

Steerable landing gear

A military Chinook has a rear cargo access ramp. However, this has been removed from the utility Chinook as it is unnecessary and would add unwanted weight

Flying at sea

Some planes operate from aircraft carriers on the ocean. They allow navies (armed forces at sea) to have their own air power, instead of depending on land aircraft for support. The US Navy's Grumman F-14 Tomcat was one of the most famous carrier aircraft and was in service from 1974 to 2006.

The Tomcat pilot had to take in a mass of data from the various dials and indicators in the cockpit.

The aircraft has twin tailfins, one on top of each exhaust nozzle

Jolly Roger symbol of fighter squadron VF-84

Variable-geometry wing changes shape for flying at different speeds

Exhaust nozzle from Pratt & Whitney jet engine

Canopy of the two-man cockpit gives good all-round vision

Variable wing in a forward position

Wing glove remains stationary while the rest of the wing rotates

Swing wings

The Tomcat had amazing moveable wings, automatically adjusted by an on-board computer. When the aircraft flew at supersonic speed, the wings swept back to almost touch the tailplane. When it came in to land, the wings moved forward to give more lift at a slower speed.

Supersonic defence

The Tomcat could fly at more than twice the speed of sound. Its main mission was to protect ships against attack. It had complex, advanced radars and targeting systems to spot enemy aircraft and guide its missiles on to them. Two crew members were needed to fly the aircraft and fight at the same time.

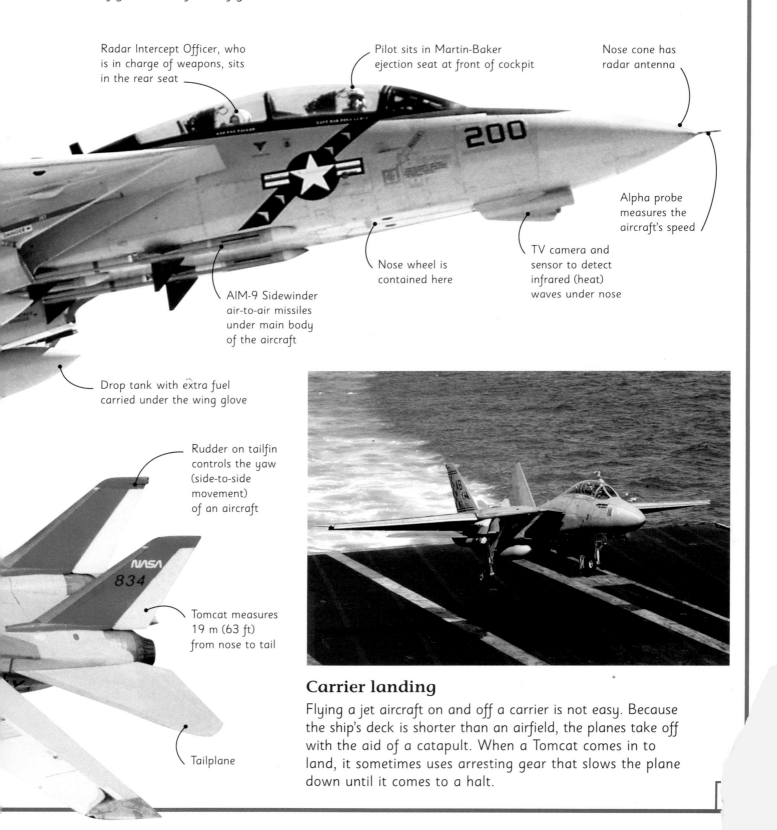

Radar Intercept Officer, who is in charge of weapons, sits in the rear seat

Pilot sits in Martin-Baker ejection seat at front of cockpit

Nose cone has radar antenna

Alpha probe measures the aircraft's speed

TV camera and sensor to detect infrared (heat) waves under nose

Nose wheel is contained here

AIM-9 Sidewinder air-to-air missiles under main body of the aircraft

Drop tank with extra fuel carried under the wing glove

Rudder on tailfin controls the yaw (side-to-side movement) of an aircraft

Tomcat measures 19 m (63 ft) from nose to tail

Tailplane

Carrier landing

Flying a jet aircraft on and off a carrier is not easy. Because the ship's deck is shorter than an airfield, the planes take off with the aid of a catapult. When a Tomcat comes in to land, it sometimes uses arresting gear that slows the plane down until it comes to a halt.

F-16

The F-16 is a multi-role fighter aircraft, originally designed for close-up air combat. It is also used for air-to-ground attack. It has excellent manoeuvrability. Flying at a height of 12 km (7.5 miles), an F-16 can reach a speed of 2,172 kph (1,350 mph) — more than twice the speed of sound. The F-16 is officially known as the Fighting Falcon, but all the pilots call it the Viper.

Raised canopy

Instructor pilot

Trainee pilot

RESCUE

U.S. FORCE

Forward landing gear

This specially adapted pitot tube is only used for flight tests

Getting ready to go

The pilots and ground crew have lots of checks to complete before they are ready to take off. These take them about 45 minutes — they check everything, including the flight controls.

The cockpit is equipped with a visual display screen known as a Heads-Up-Display. It tells the pilots where they are and displays weapons and targeting information

Pitot tube

RESCUE

MAJ. ROB ADAM

A bright yellow arrow points to a handle. Ground crew members pull this to pop open the canopy in an emergency

The first F-16s had black radomes (or radar covers). Pilots felt it was an easy target for enemy fire, so the black was changed to grey

The forward landing gear retracts into a compartment in flight

The F-16 is the most commonly used aircraft in the US Air Force. It is also used in many other countries.

The F-16 has a unique flight control system known as fly-by-wire. It means that computers and electronics have replaced many of the older-style mechanical workings

A gaping hole?

The positioning of the air intake under the cockpit's canopy is unusual. The F-16 was designed like this to avoid the intake being affected by the high angles the plane achieves while twisting and turning in flight.

The ejection seat will eject the pilot in an emergency in less than one second

The bubble canopy provides excellent vision for the pilots

Low-sweep straight wing

Horizontal stabilisers on each side move in flight

The nose is packed with radar equipment

Heat-seeking missiles or radar-guided missiles can be clipped to the tips of the wings

The pull of the air intake is so strong that it would suck in a person if they stood too close to it

Chocks are left under the wheels when the F-16 is stationary

In the hot seat

This two-seater F-16 is a trainer plane – a student pilot sits in the front and an instructor takes the rear seat. They wear G-suits to prevent blood loss from the head into the lower parts of their bodies, which could cause them to blackout. The suit squeezes the lower part of the body to "push" the blood back up to the brain.

Navigation light

A recovery parachute container is located behind each seat

The F-16 can be refuelled in-flight at this point

AF 78 098

ED

Tailfin with identifying registration

U.S. AIR FORCE

Exhaust nozzle

Fixed ventral fin, used for improving stability at high speed

Landing gear compartment hatch

Red ribbons are removed before flight

In flight, the main undercarriage retracts into the fuselage

Seaplane

Seaplanes are fitted with floats instead of wheels, so they can take off or land wherever there is a flat stretch of water. They are mostly used in areas that have few airfields but plenty of lakes, rivers, or calm coastal seas.

Green starboard light

Which side is which?

Like boats, aeroplanes have a red port light on the left side and a green starboard light on the right side. At night, these lights help to identify which direction the plane is facing.

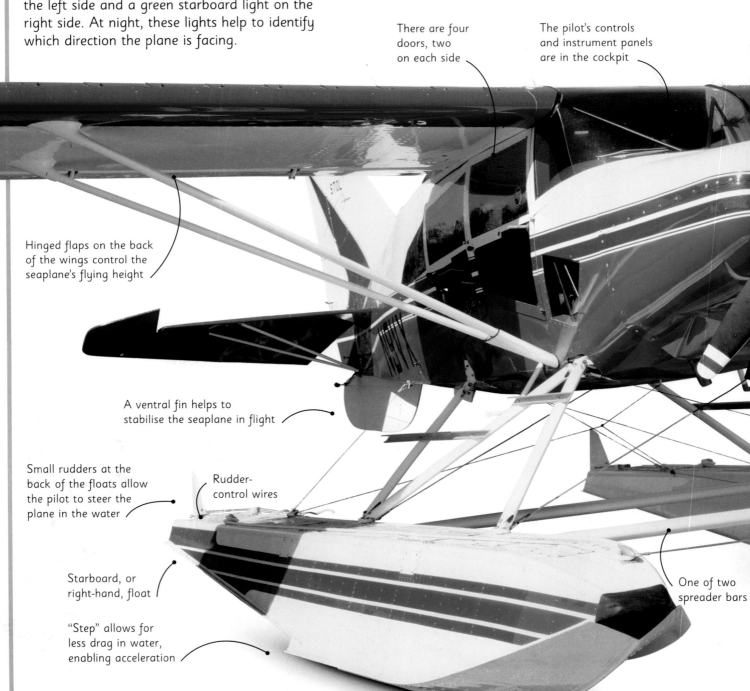

There are four doors, two on each side

The pilot's controls and instrument panels are in the cockpit

Hinged flaps on the back of the wings control the seaplane's flying height

A ventral fin helps to stabilise the seaplane in flight

Small rudders at the back of the floats allow the pilot to steer the plane in the water

Rudder-control wires

Starboard, or right-hand, float

"Step" allows for less drag in water, enabling acceleration

One of two spreader bars

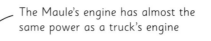

The Maule's engine has almost the same power as a truck's engine

A water taxi

This little seaplane is a Maule. It is a popular craft for carrying small groups of people, rather like a taxi carries people from place to place on the road. It can carry three passengers and a pilot.

Wing lift strut

Struts support the plane on its floats

The spreader bar holds the floats rigid in flight and in the water

Exhaust pipe

Like boats, the floats take in water and have to be pumped out

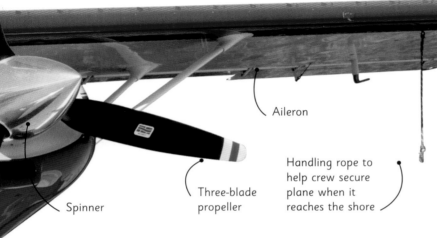

Aileron

Handling rope to help crew secure plane when it reaches the shore

Spinner

Three-blade propeller

Landing on water

Once the pilot has landed, he or she has to taxi forward very slowly. This prevents spray from the bow wave from damaging the propeller. However, the plane has to move fast enough to allow the rudders on the floats to work. It's a skilful job to get it right.

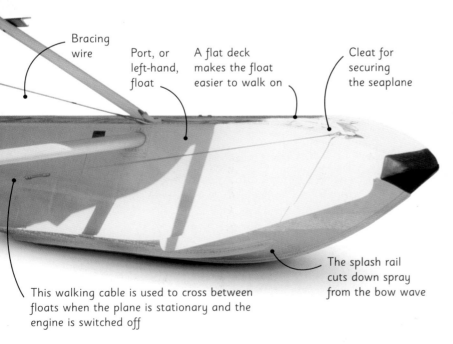

Bracing wire

Port, or left-hand, float

A flat deck makes the float easier to walk on

Cleat for securing the seaplane

The splash rail cuts down spray from the bow wave

This walking cable is used to cross between floats when the plane is stationary and the engine is switched off

A seaplane can land in a sheltered harbour, river, or lake. It needs about 1.6 km (1 mile) of clear water as its "runway".

Stealth fighter

The Lockheed F-117 Nighthawk was the world's first successful "stealth" aircraft. It was designed to be almost invisible to radar – a device that sends out radio waves to detect a moving object. Coated in a special black material that absorbs radio waves, it looked like an aeroplane out of fantasy fiction, but it worked. At night, the F-117 could fly into enemy territory as if wearing an invisibility cloak.

Out of sight

The Nighthawk entered service with the US Air Force in 1983. With a maximum speed of 1,040 kph (646 mph), it was slower than other warplanes. Its ability to stay hidden was the main reason it could survive in battle.

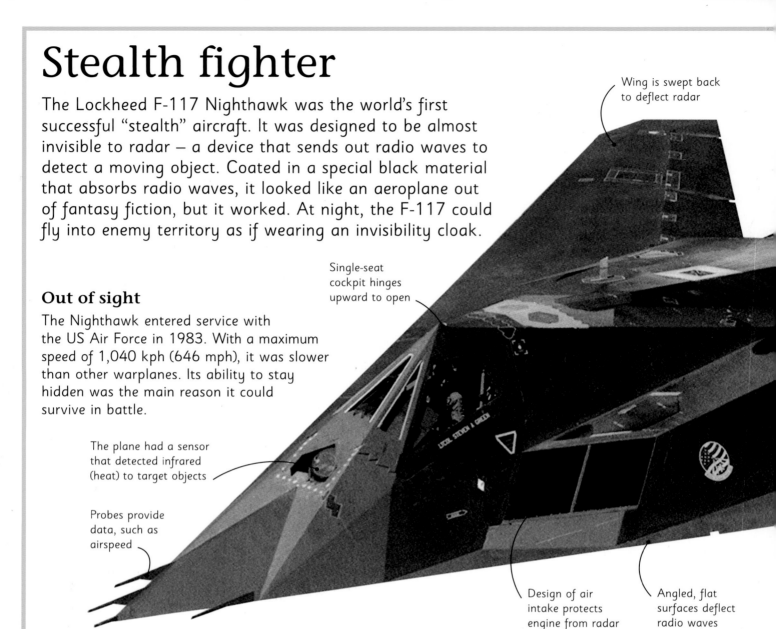

Wing is swept back to deflect radar

Single-seat cockpit hinges upward to open

The plane had a sensor that detected infrared (heat) to target objects

Probes provide data, such as airspeed

Design of air intake protects engine from radar

Angled, flat surfaces deflect radio waves

Give me a brake!

Because of its odd design, the Nighthawk had a high landing speed of around 300 kph (185 mph). Once it hit the runway, a parachute brake was released to slow it down and bring it to a stop.

Razor-thin wing edge minimizes radar reflection

Hinged sections on the V-shaped tail, called a ruddervator, act as rudder and elevator

V-tail functions as tailfin and tailplane

Exhaust nozzle edged with tiles that provide protection from extreme heat

Exhaust is slit-shaped to reduce infrared emissions that can be detected by the enemy

To honour the aircraft's retirement from service in 2008, two Nighthawks flew with the US flag painted on their underside.

Wingspan is 13 m (43 ft)

The pilot had a very limited view from the cockpit

Vent through which air is pulled into the plane's turbofan engine

Shaped like a diamond

In addition to the plane's outer coating that absorbed radio waves, each angle of the F-117's surfaces was precisely calculated to scatter radar waves. All its weapons were carried inside the main body. Although known as a fighter plane, it was mostly used to attack targets on the ground and not to fight other aircraft.

Wings and aircraft body make a single surface

Nose wheel retracts forwards

Main wheels disappear into the main body during flight

Moveable flaps on the wings, called elevons, control how the plane rotates from side to side, and from the tip to tail

Space flight

The first person flew into space in 1961. Since then astronauts have walked on the Moon and been on space stations that orbit the Earth, while space probes have explored the far reaches of the solar system. Today, SpaceX Dragon, a free-flying, reusable spacecraft, represents the best of cutting-edge space travel technology in the 21st century.

The Dragon spacecraft is launched into orbit atop a two-stage Falcon 9 rocket. The Falcon has a total of 10 rocket engines.

Solar cells use the Sun's rays to provide energy for onboard systems

The Dragon craft

The SpaceX Dragon is an unmanned vehicle that carries cargo to and from the International Space Station (ISS). It consists of a pressurized capsule and unpressurized trunk. The capsule is reusable. It re-enters the atmosphere protected by a heat shield, and makes a soft landing on the Earth.

Trunk hold has a capacity for 14 cubic m (490 cubic ft) of cargo

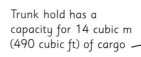

Docked in space

A Dragon spacecraft first docked at the International Space Station in 2012. Docking means attaching one spacecraft with another in space. Remote-controlled thrusters move the spacecraft to docking. A robotic arm from the space station secures the Dragon while cargo is loaded and unloaded through a hatch, or small opening, in the capsule's nose.

Advanced capsule

The Dragon's pressurized capsule is fully suitable for manned flight. A manned version of the spacecraft, the Crew Dragon, is planned to act as a replacement for the Space Shuttle. It is expected to be ready to carry up to seven crew or passengers by 2018.

Cone protecting top of capsule is jettisoned after launch

Docking hatch links capsule to space station

Pressurized capsule carries cargo and, potentially, crew

Draco thrusters move the capsule

Advanced PICA-X heat shield protects capsule on re-entry

Unpressurized trunk carries cargo and houses solar panels

Height of vehicle with its trunk is 7 m (23 ft)

Frame supports capsule when it's out of service

Solar arrays unfold from trunk in space

Solar panels are ditched along with the trunk before re-entry

Record breakers

In the continual search for improved performance, aeroplanes have become increasingly high-tech. Here are some of the amazing flying machines that have set outstanding records.

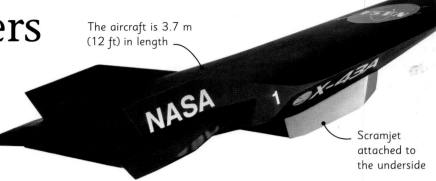

The aircraft is 3.7 m (12 ft) in length

Scramjet attached to the underside

Fastest unmanned aeroplane

NASA's X-43A, an unmanned experimental aircraft, reached 7,564 mph (12,144 kph) in 2004, becoming the fastest jet aeroplane ever. Only rockets travel faster.

Roomy hold for cargo or troops

Biggest helicopter

The largest helicopter ever to enter production is the Russian Mil Mi-26. Used for military transport, it can carry 90 soldiers. Its rotors are 32 m (105 ft) in diameter.

Largest, heaviest, and longest

The Ukrainian Antonov An-225 Mriya transport plane is the world's biggest aircraft in length, wingspan, and weight. Powered by six turbofan engines, its maximum takeoff weight is 640,000 kg (1.4 million lbs).

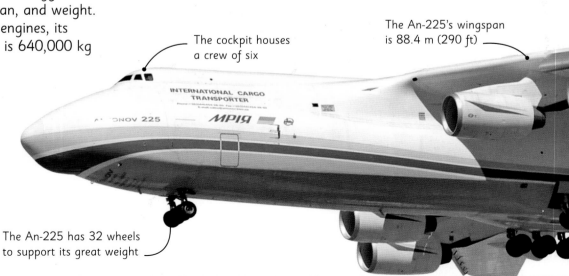

The cockpit houses a crew of six

The An-225's wingspan is 88.4 m (290 ft)

The An-225 has 32 wheels to support its great weight

Highest flyer

SpaceShipOne achieved the record altitude for a manned aeroplane in October 2004, flying 112 km (70 miles) high, to the edge of the Earth's atmosphere. A mother ship (carrier-aircraft) called the White Knight was used to launch SpaceShipOne.

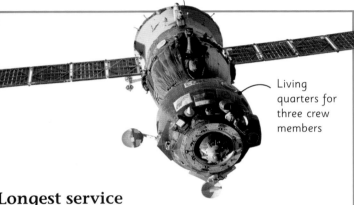

SpaceShipOne ready for air launch

White Knight carrier ship lifts SpaceShipOne to an altitude of 15 km (10 miles)

Starboard fuselage of White Knight

Living quarters for three crew members

Longest service

In service from 1967, the Russian Soyuz spacecraft has not had an accident since 1971. By 2015, it had flown on more than 120 missions. It is the most reliable, longest-serving, and safest space vehicle.

Quickest helicopter

The official record for the fastest-ever helicopter flight is held by a specially adapted British Westland Lynx that flew at 401 kph (249 mph) in 1986.

G-LYNX

Tube-shaped landing skids

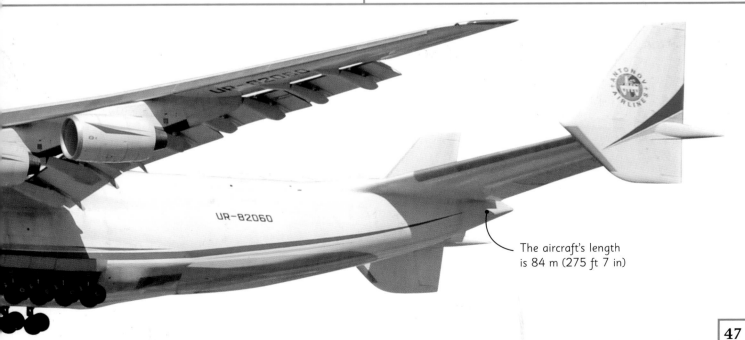

UR-82060

The aircraft's length is 84 m (275 ft 7 in)

Glossary

aerial Wire or rod that sticks out from an object to pick up radio waves

aerodynamic Shape designed to cut through air smoothly and cleanly

aileron Flap close to a plane's wingtip that is used to control the rolling motion of a plane

air intake Place where air is taken into a machine. Air is needed to mix with fuel to make an engine go

altitude Height of an object above land or sea level

avionics Aircraft's electronic and navigation equipment

ejection seat Seat that contains an explosive charge and a parachute. It can be ejected from an aeroplane in an emergency to save the pilot

elevator Flat control surface that is used to make a plane climb or dive

exhaust Pipe through which waste fumes are pushed out from an engine

fuselage Body of an aircraft

horsepower Measure of an engine's power. One unit of horsepower is loosely based on the power of a horse

hypersonic Plane travelling at more than five times the speed of sound

infrared Type of radiation given off by hot objects. It is invisible to the eye, but special sensors can detect it

jet engine All engines need fuel and oxygen to make them go. A "jet" engine uses a jet of air for extra thrust

landing gear Wheels of an aeroplane

pitot tube Pipe that sticks out from an aircraft and measures air speed

port Left-hand side of a ship or aeroplane

radar Means of detecting objects that are not within sight by bouncing radio waves off them

rocket engine Type of jet engine that carries the oxygen it needs in a tank

rudder Hinged flap at the back of the plane that is used to turn an aircraft to the left or right

speed of sound Sound travels at about 1,224 kph (760 mph)

starboard Right-hand side of a ship or aeroplane

supersonic Plane that flies faster than the speed of sound

thermal protection External coating or covering that protects an aeroplane from too much heat

undercarriage Landing gear of an aircraft

Index